# ANCIENT GREECE FOR KIDS

## HISTORY, ART, WAR, CULTURE, SOCIETY AND MORE
## ANCIENT GREECE ENCYCLOPEDIA
## 5TH GRADE SOCIAL STUDIES

Speedy Publishing LLC

40 E. Main St. #1156

Newark, DE 19711

www.speedypublishing.com

Copyright 2017

In this book, we're going to talk all about Ancient Greece. So, let's get right to it!

Thousands of years ago, when the civilization of Ancient Greece was at its peak, it was the dominant country in the Mediterranean area. Under the leadership of Alexander the Great, the country of Greece was in control of most of Europe as well as regions of Western Asia. The Roman Empire followed the Greeks and their culture was largely adopted from Grecian culture since they greatly admired the Greeks. In fact, much of Western culture was directly influenced by ancient Greece.

ATHENS, GREECE

ANCIENT ACROPOLIS

# HISTORY

Historians study Ancient Greece by dividing it into three major time periods.

# THE ARCHAIC PERIOD

This period spanned the time when the civilization was first established circa 800 BC to when the principles of Democracy were introduced around 508 BC. The Olympics were started in this era of Greece's history.

ERECHTHEION TEMPLE

HOMER

Homer, the Greek author, wrote some of the most famous works of antiquity, The Odyssey, which was about the adventures of Odysseus, and The Iliad, which was about the last part of the Trojan War.

# THE CLASSICAL PERIOD

This period is perhaps the most famous in Greek history. The great Greek philosopher Socrates and his pupil Plato were teaching during this era. The city-state of Athens was already being governed using the principles of democracy.

ATHENS, GREECE

ALEXANDER THE GREAT

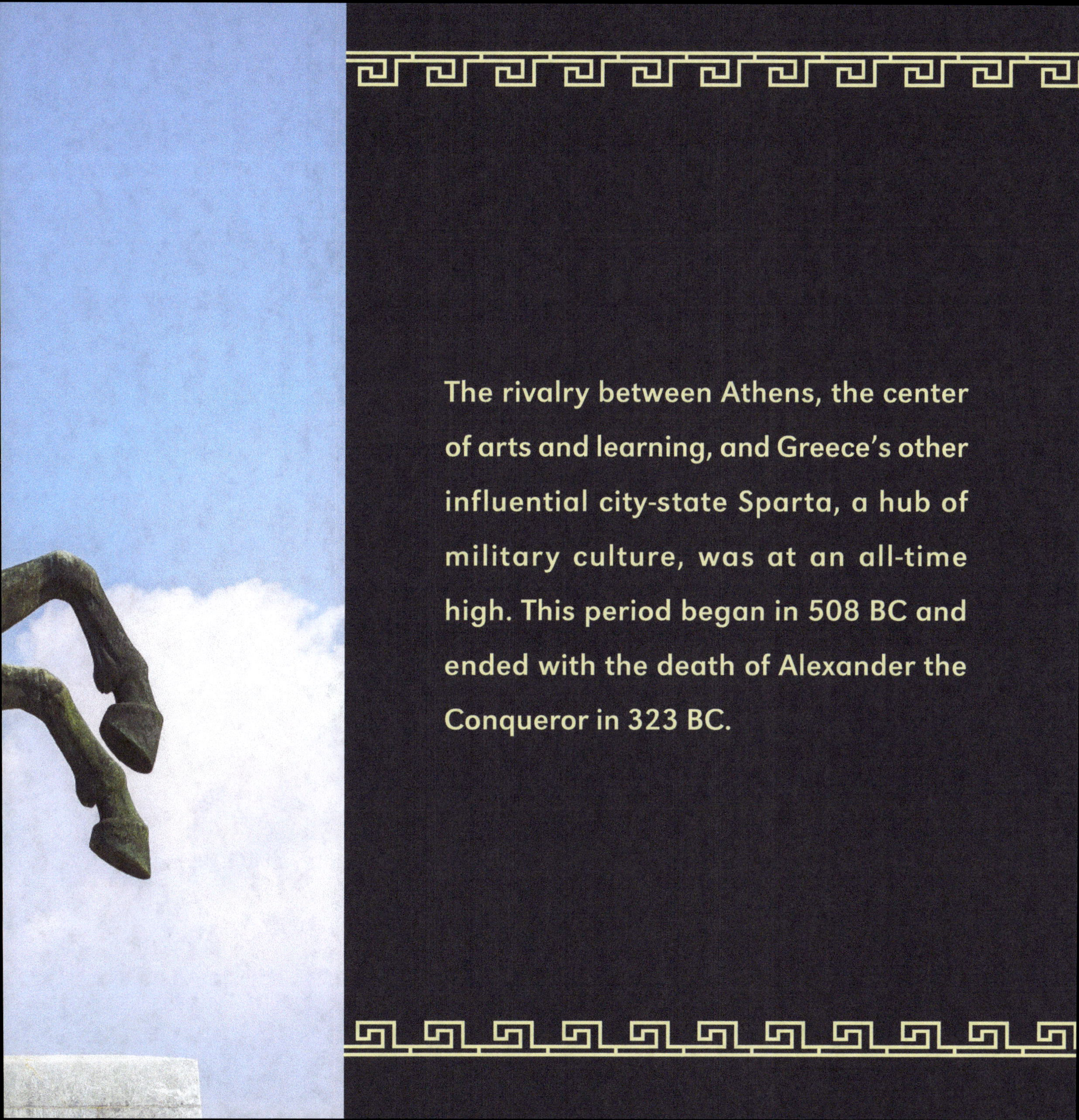

The rivalry between Athens, the center of arts and learning, and Greece's other influential city-state Sparta, a hub of military culture, was at an all-time high. This period began in 508 BC and ended with the death of Alexander the Conqueror in 323 BC.

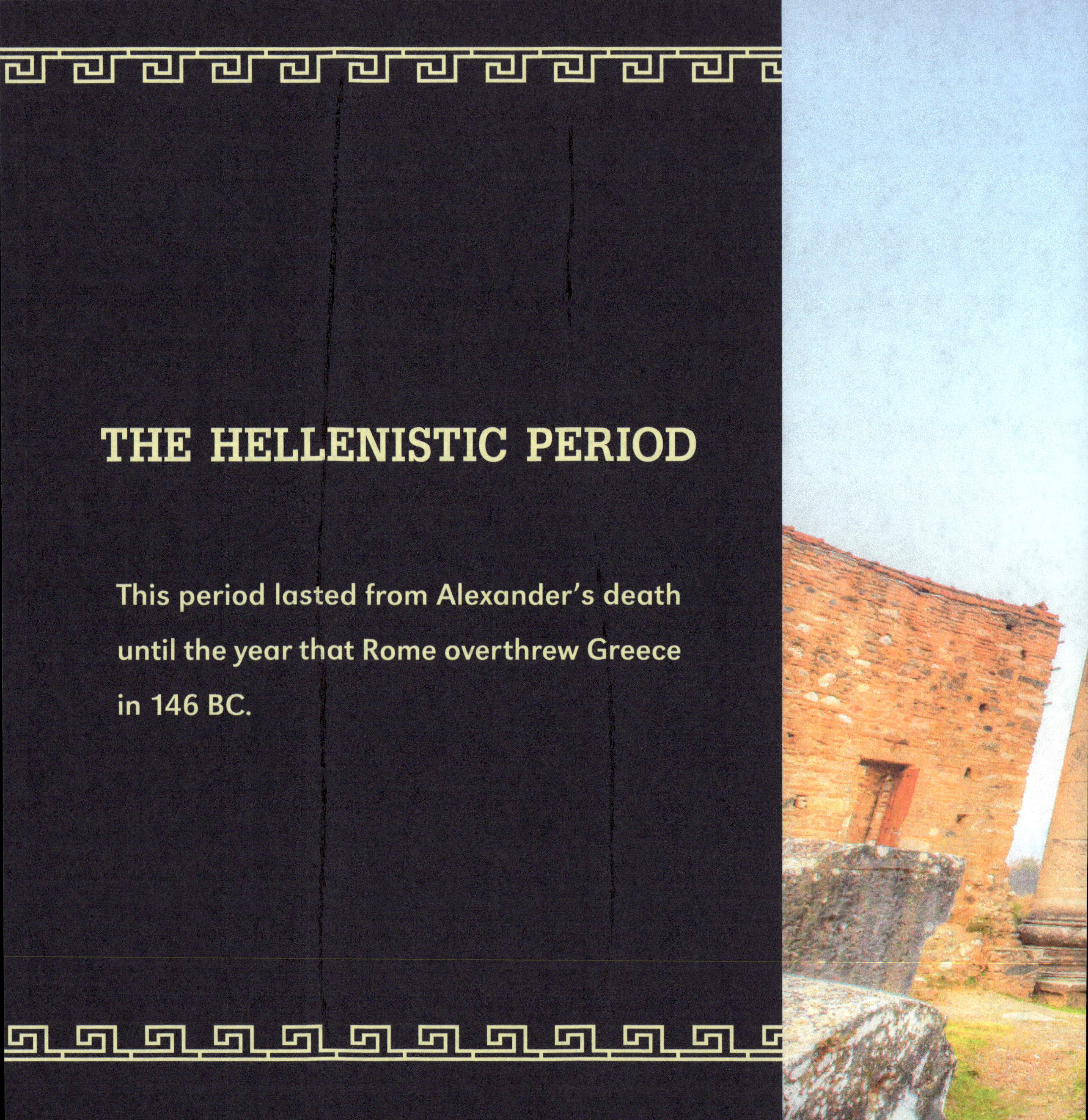

# THE HELLENISTIC PERIOD

This period lasted from Alexander's death until the year that Rome overthrew Greece in 146 BC.

TEMPLE OF ARTEMIS

GREEK GODDESS MARBLE STATUE

# ART

The Greeks became known throughout the world for their mastery of artistic expression. The Greeks wanted their art to represent the ideal perfection of beauty.

During the Archaic Period, the Greeks created sculptures, primarily of men and women. The sculptures of males were described as Kouroi and the sculptures of females were described as Korai. They had similar-looking facial features and their postures were rather stiff with their arms held close to their torsos.

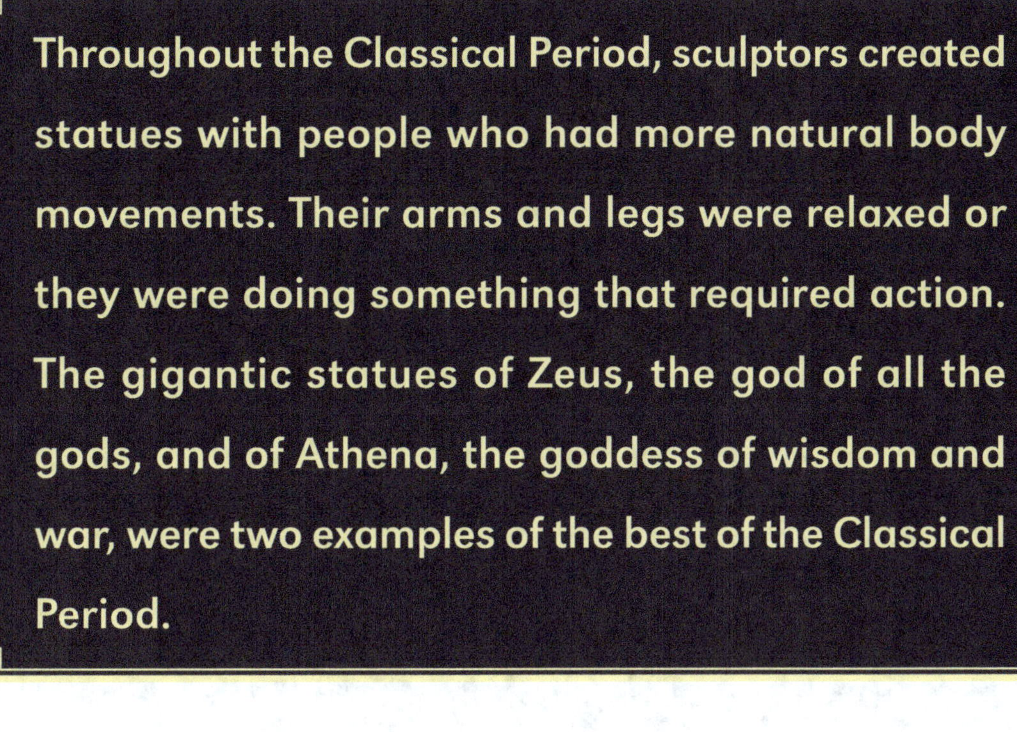

Throughout the Classical Period, sculptors created statues with people who had more natural body movements. Their arms and legs were relaxed or they were doing something that required action. The gigantic statues of Zeus, the god of all the gods, and of Athena, the goddess of wisdom and war, were two examples of the best of the Classical Period.

During the Hellenistic Period, Grecian art was heavily influenced by the other populations that Alexander the Great had conquered. Mortal women and children were frequent art subjects. Up until this time period, ordinary people weren't depicted in art. The Winged Victory is a famous sculpture from this time period as is the Venus de Milo.

VENUS DE MILO

# ARCHITECTURE

The unique architecture that the Greeks designed is still used for construction all over the world today. Some of the characteristics of Greek buildings were their tall distinct columns and the overall effect of harmonious symmetry and balance.

The Greeks designed three types of columns. The Doric column was thick with no base decoration and a simple design for the top, which was called the capital of the column. The Ionic column was a thinner design than the Doric. Its capital was adorned with a scroll design on both sides. The Corinthian column was the most highly decorated of the three types of columns. It had scrolls and leaves from a plant called the acanthus. This last style was used at the end of the Hellenistic era and was copied by the Romans.

ALEXANDER THE GREAT

# WAR

Beginning around 500 BC, Greece fought the Empire of Persia. At that time, Persia was a vast empire that had domain of much of the land surrounding the Mediterranean Sea. Their empire extended from Egypt to what we know as modern-day India. It took many battles over more than a century of time, but when Alexander the Great and his army fought, they eventually defeated the Persians in 333 BC.

The city-states of Athens and Sparta, both within Greece, were always at war with each other. The rivals fought a long and intense war, the Peloponnesian War, from 431 BC to 404 BC. Sparta, the more warlike of the two rivals, won this war.

RUINS OF THE ANCIENT GREEK CITY OF SPARTA

ANCIENT GREEK THEATER ODEON OF HERODES ATTICUS IN ATHENS

# CULTURE AND SOCIETY

The men in Greek society spent much of their time training for the military. They also spent hours talking about politics and attending the theater, which was invented by the Greeks, for entertainment. Their dramas and comedies frequently centered around politics or the mythology of their gods and goddesses. Men actors played the roles for women since women weren't allowed to participate in the theater or watch the performances.

Men in Greece had many different occupations. Some were farmers and fishermen. Many belonged to the military at different levels or were government workers. Men were merchants, craftsmen, and teachers.

IXMII
ANCIENT SOLDIERS

Women did most of the domestic work. They created the fabric for clothes by spinning and weaving. They raised the children and handled the cooking.

THE TEMPLE OF ZEUS WITH THE ANDRON

The Andron was the part of the house that was just for men. They used it to have dinner parties for their friends and business associates. This room had the most beautiful furniture in the house. As they enjoyed their evening meal served by slaves, they talked about philosophy or politics. After dinner they would drink a mixture of water and wine.

RUINED HOUSE IN ANCIENT APTERA, GREECE

The women of the house weren't allowed in this room. They had a similar room upstairs where they could receive their friends and family members. It wasn't as luxurious as the men's room and it was called the Gynaikon. They often did their spinning and weaving there as they talked together and watched over the children.

# GODS AND GODDESSES

The Greeks believed in numerous gods and goddesses.

The Greeks constructed temples and offered sacrifices to them. They believed that the twelve major gods and goddesses lived on Mount Olympus.

ZEUS

Zeus was the leader and he was the god of the sky, thunder, and lightning. He was married to his sister, Hera, who was the goddess of marriage. When the Romans took over the Greek civilization, they adopted many of the same gods and goddesses and simply renamed them. There were hundreds of myths about the gods and goddesses, and their epic adventures and battles. They were just like people in many ways. They had strengths and weaknesses, but they also had superhuman powers.

# PHILOSOPHY

The Greek philosophers loved wisdom and they sought the truth by exploring important questions about life and the nature of mankind. Socrates derived a question and answer method of learning that we still use today. The questions in his method were open-ended and designed to make you think so that you would be motivated to find the answers for yourself. His method was eventually named after him and called the Socratic method.

SOCRATES

Although Socrates didn't document his work in writing, his student Plato did. He wrote down his mentor's work in dialogues where Socrates was the teacher.

PLATO

In these conversations, Plato describes the ideal society as envisioned by Socrates. Aristotle was one of Plato's students. He was an advocate for logical reasoning and tied much of his philosophy to science.

ARISTOTLE

# SPORTS

The Olympic Games that we have today were started by the Greeks about 3,000 years ago around 776 BC.

The games were held every four years in the month of August until around 393 AD when they were banned by Theodosius, the Christian Roman Emperor. The modern Olympics that we have today was re-established in 1896 by Pierre de Coubertin, a French educator.

The games were originally designed to honor the Greek god Zeus, the ruler of all the Greek gods on Mount Olympus. At the start, the games were foot races of short lengths. The men ran the 700-foot long track with twenty of them side by side. They competed with no clothes on. Eventually, other events, such as spear and disc throwing and the long jump, were added. At its height, about 40,000 people attended the Ancient Olympics.

ZEUS

# ANCIENT GREECE HAS A COLORFUL HISTORY

Thousands of years ago, Ancient Greece was the dominant Mediterranean country. They created innovations in all aspects of culture. Their presence is still felt today. In fact, it would be difficult to go through any day in Western society without coming into contact with words, philosophical principles, entertainment, or art that originated from the culture of Ancient Greece.

Awesome! Now that you've read about ancient Greece, you may want to read more about the art of ancient Greece in the Baby Professor book The Severe Style of Ancient Greek Art – Art History for Kids | Children's Art Books.

Visit

BABY PROFESSOR
EDUCATION KIDS

www.BabyProfessorBooks.com

to download Free Baby Professor eBooks
and view our catalog of new and exciting
Children's Books